50 *Fabulous* Knit Garter Stitches

by Rita Weiss

Leisure Arts, Inc.
Little Rock, Arkansas

Produced by

Production Team

Creative Directors: Jean Leinhauser and
Rita Weiss

Technical Editor: Ellen W. Liberles

Photographer: Carol Wilson Mansfield

Pattern Tester: Kimberly Britt

Book Design: Linda Causee

Published by Leisure Arts

© 2010 by Leisure Arts, Inc.,
5701 Ranch Drive
Little Rock, AR 72223
www.leisurearts.com

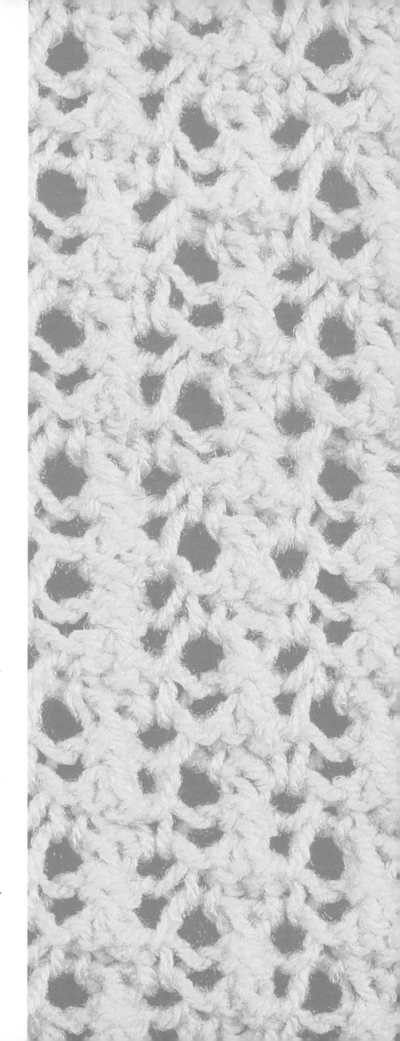

Introduction

Garter stitch is the first stitch you learn when someone teaches you to knit, but rows and rows of just a knit stitch are pretty boring. So to most people garter stitch itself is boring, just a knit stitch followed by another knit stitch.

Is garter stitch not as interesting or as creative as stockinette stitch that uses the knit stitch with a purl stitch?

Wrong. Garter stitch has many dimensions and many disguises. Garter stitch can be used to make lace, ripples, mosaic designs, ribbings. In fact, without using a purl stitch, garter stitch can even be made to look just like stockinette.

So here is a collection of 50 different stitches all created by only using a knit stitch! There are no purl stitches in this book, but you'll find a wonderful collection of fabulous patterns. They are fun to make and will add a new dimension to your knitting.

You won't find any reference to gauge in this book because you can work these stitches with any type of yarn or thread you choose. Try one of the lacy stitches with the finest lace weight fiber to produce the most delicate of lace with just a knit stitch. Want to make a heavy sweater or an afghan, choose another of the stitches and a worsted or bulky weight yarn.

What you will find here is the word "multiple" at the start of each stitch pattern. A multiple is the number of stitches needed to work one complete unit of the pattern. If the pattern says "Multiple: 3 + 2", you will need to cast on any number of stitches which can be evenly divided by 3: 6, 9, 11, 15, 18 or 21 for example. To this you must add the "+2" so that you will cast on 2 more stitches to the total giving for example 8, 11, 14, 17, 20 or 23 stitches. It is important to remember that the "+" number is added just once.

And believe it or not, this is the last time you'll see the word "purl" in this book.

Contents

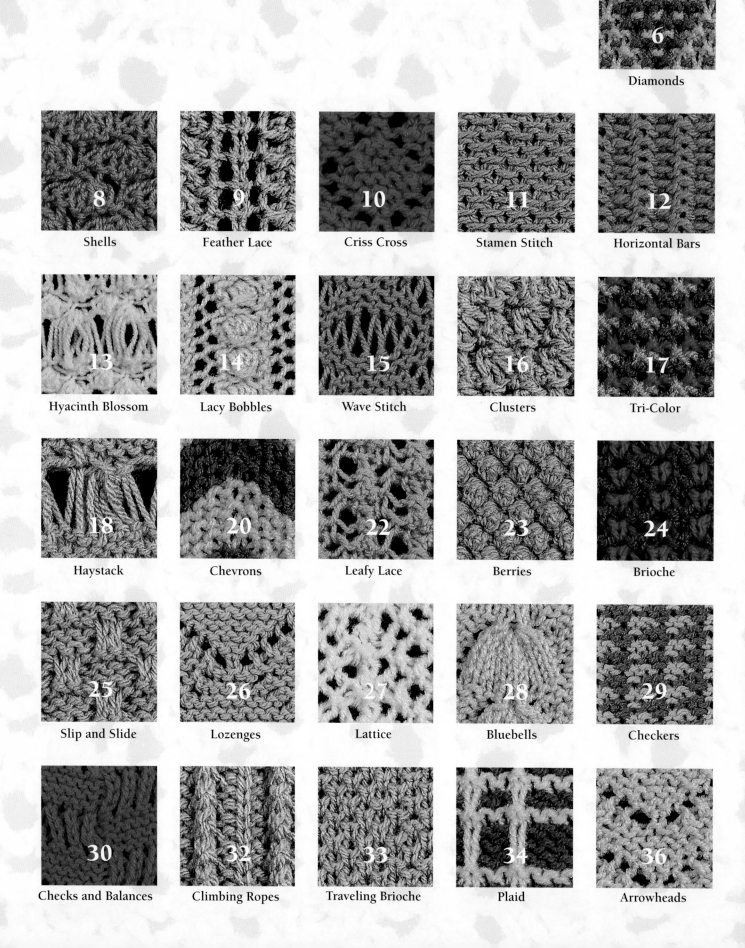

Open Ribs

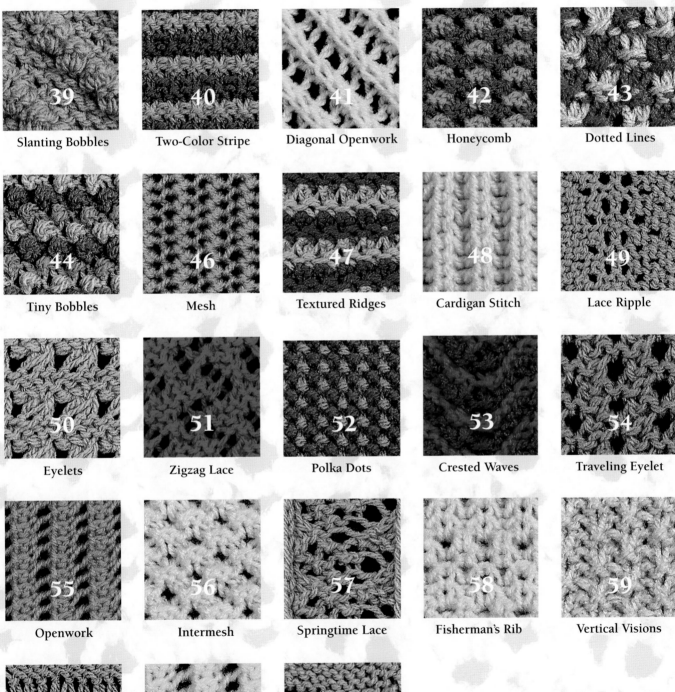

39 Slanting Bobbles	**40** Two-Color Stripe	**41** Diagonal Openwork	**42** Honeycomb	**43** Dotted Lines
44 Tiny Bobbles	**46** Mesh	**47** Textured Ridges	**48** Cardigan Stitch	**49** Lace Ripple
50 Eyelets	**51** Zigzag Lace	**52** Polka Dots	**53** Crested Waves	**54** Traveling Eyelet
55 Openwork	**56** Intermesh	**57** Springtime Lace	**58** Fisherman's Rib	**59** Vertical Visions
60 Drop Stitch	**61** Eyelet Columns	**62** Garter Cockle Shells		

General Directions 64

Diamonds

Multiple: 10 + 3

INSTRUCTIONS

Two Colors: *Color A and Color B; carry unused color loosely along side.*

Row 1 (right side): With A, K1; *sl 1, K9; rep from * to last 2 sts, sl 1, K1.

Row 2: K1; *YF, sl 1, YB, K9; rep from * to last 2 sts, YF, sl 1, YB, K1.

Row 3: With B, K3; *(sl 1, K1) 3 times, sl 1, K3; rep from * across.

Row 4: K3; *(YF, sl 1, YB, K1) 3 times, YF, sl 1, K3 rep from * across.

Row 5: With A, K2; *sl 1, K7, sl 1, K1; rep from * to last st, K1.

Row 6: K2; *YF, sl 1, YB, K7, YF, sl 1, YB, K1; rep from * to last st, K1.

Row 7: With B, *K4, (sl 1, K1) 3 times; rep from * to last 3 sts, K3.

Row 8: K4, (YF, sl 1, YB, K1) twice, YF, sl 1, YB, *K5, (YF, sl 1, YB, K1) twice, YF, sl 1; rep from * to last 4 sts, K4.

Row 9: With A, (K1, sl 1) twice; *K5, (sl 1, K1) twice, sl 1; rep from * to last 9 sts, K5, (sl 1, K1) twice.

Row 10: (K1, YF, sl 1, YB) twice; *K5, (YF, sl 1, YB, K1) twice, YF, sl 1, YB; rep from * to last 9 sts, K5, (YF, sl 1, YB, K1) twice.

Row 11: With B, K5, sl 1, K1, sl 1; *K7, sl 1, K1, sl 1; rep from * to last 5 sts, K5.

Row 12: K5, YF, sl 1, YB, K1, YF, sl 1, YB; *K7, YF, sl 1, YB, K1, YF, sl 1; rep from * to last 5 sts, K5.

Row 13: With A, K2, sl 1, K1, sl 1, K3; *(sl 1, K1) 3 times, sl 1, K3; rep from * to last 5 sts, sl 1, K1, sl 1, K2.

Row 14: K2, YF, sl 1, YB, K1, YF, sl 1, YB, K3; *(YF, sl 1, YB, K1) 3 times, YF, sl 1, YB, K3; rep from * to last 5 sts, YF, sl 1, YB, K1, YF, sl 1, YB, K2.

Row 15: With B, K6; *sl 1, K9; rep from * to last 7 sts, sl 1, K6.

Row 16: K6; *YF, sl 1, YB, K9; rep from * to last 7 sts, YF, sl 1, YB, K6.

Row 17: Rep Row 9.

Row 18: Rep Row 10.

Row 19: Rep Row 11.

Row 20: Rep Row 12.

Row 21: Rep Row 5.

Row 22: Rep Row 6.

Row 23: Rep Row 7.

Row 24: Rep Row 8.

Repeat Rows 1 through 24 for pattern, ending by working Rows 1 and 2.

Shells

Multiple: 8 + 3, having at least 19 sts

STITCH GUIDE

K1(W2): K1, wrapping yarn twice around needle.

P2SSO: pass 2 sl sts over K3tog st.

Inc (Increase): Knit into front then back lp of YO.

Inc (Increase) in K1 (W2): Knit into knit st, then knit into front and back lp of YO: 3 sts made in 2 lps.

INSTRUCTIONS

Row 1: K1; *YO, K1; rep from * across.

Row 2 (right side): Knit, dropping all YOs off needle.

Row 3: K1, K3tog; *K1(W2), K1, K1(W2), sl 2, K3tog, P2SSO; rep from * to last 7 sts, K1(W2), K1, K1(W2), K3tog, K1.

Row 4: K1; *Inc in K1 (W2), rep from * to last 2 sts, K2.

Row 5: Rep Row 1.

Row 6: Rep Row 2.

Row 7: K1; *K1, K1(W2), sl 2, K3tog, P2SSO, K1(W2); rep from * to last 2 sts, K2.

Row 8: Repeat Row 4.

Repeat Rows 1 through 8 for pattern.

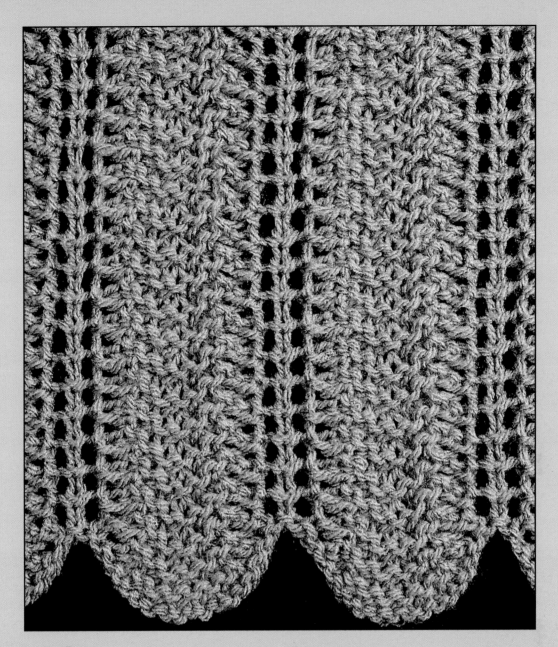

Feather Lace

Multiple 18+2

INSTRUCTIONS

Row 1: Knit.

Row 2 (right side): K1; *(K2tog) 3 times, (YO, K1) 6 times, (K2tog) 3 times; rep from * to last st, K1.

Repeat Rows 1 and 2 for pattern.

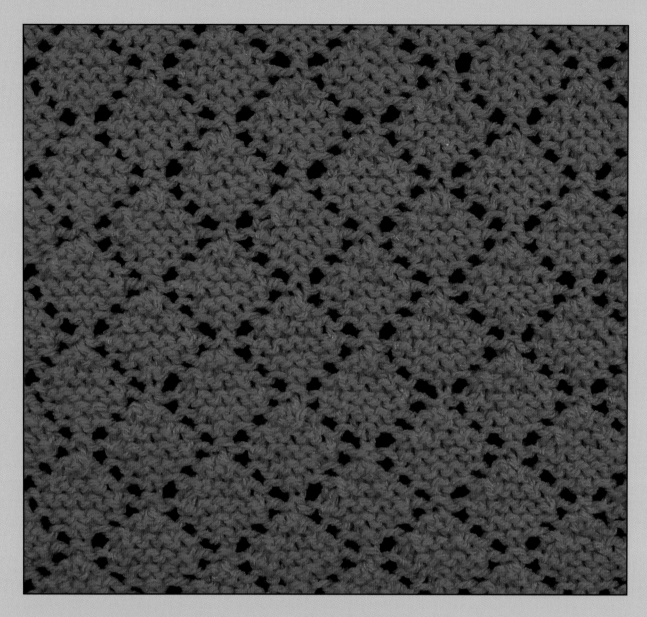

Criss Cross

Multiple: 8 + 5

INSTRUCTIONS

Row 1 (right side): K4; *K2tog, YO, K1, YO, K2tog, K3; rep from * to last st, K1.

Row 2 and all even rows: Knit.

Row 3: K3; *K2tog, YO, K3, YO, K2tog, K1; rep from * to last 2 sts, K2.

Row 5: K2, K2tog; *YO, K5, YO, sl 1, K2tog, PSSO; rep from * to last 4 sts, YO, K2tog, K2.

Row 7: K3; *YO, K2tog, K3, K2tog, YO, K1; rep from * to last 2 sts, K2.

Row 9: K4; *YO, K2tog, K1, K2tog, YO, K3; rep from * to last st, K1.

Row 11: K5; *YO, sl 1, K2tog, PSSO, YO, K5; rep from * across.

Row 12: Rep Row 2.

Repeat Rows 1 through 12 for pattern.

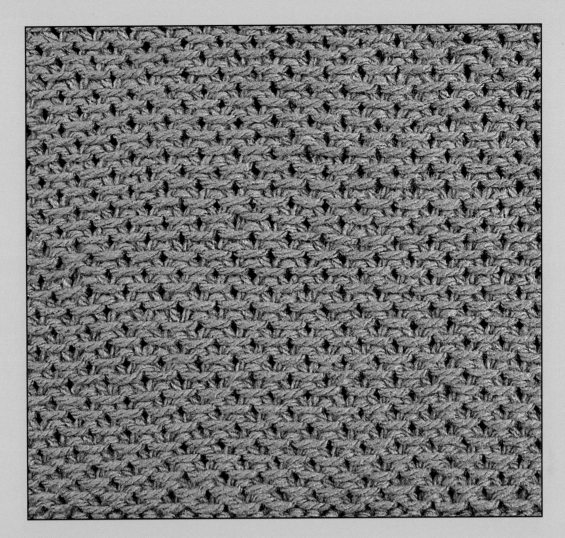

Stamen Stitch

Multiple: 2

INSTRUCTIONS

Row 1 (right side): Knit.

Row 2: *K1, sl 1; rep from * to last 2 sts, K2.

Row 3: Knit.

Row 4: K2; *sl 1, K1; rep from * across.

Repeat Rows 1 through 4 for pattern.

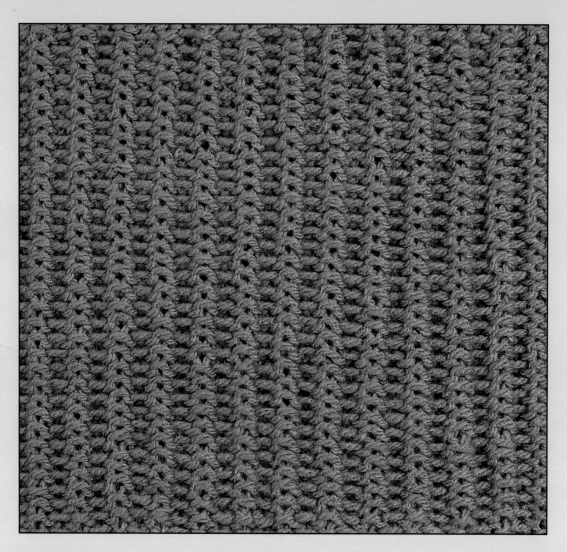

Horizontal Bars

Multiple: 3 + 2

INSTRUCTIONS

Row 1: Knit.

Row 2 (right side): K1; *K1, YF, sl 2 sts,
YB; rep from * to last st, K1.

Repeat Rows 1 and 2 for pattern.

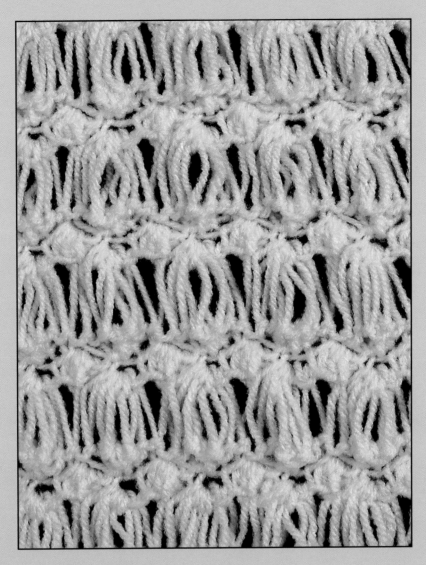

Hyacinth Blossom

Multiple: 6 + 2

STITCH GUIDE

M5 (Make 5): K1, K1tbl, YO, K1, K1tbl in same st: 5 sts worked in one st.

P4SSO: Pass 4 sl sts over knit stitch.

K1(W3): K1, wrapping yarn aound needle three times.

INSTRUCTIONS

Row 1 (wrong side): K1; *YF, sl 4, YB, K1, P4SSO, M5; rep from * to last st, K1.

Row 2: Knit.

Row 3: K1; *M5, YF, sl 4, YB, K1, P4SSO; rep from * to last st, K1.

Row 4: Knit.

Row 5: K1; *K1(W3); rep from * to last st, K1.

Row 6: Knit each st, allowing all YOs to drop.

Rep Rows 1 through 6 for pattern, ending by working Rows 1 through 4.

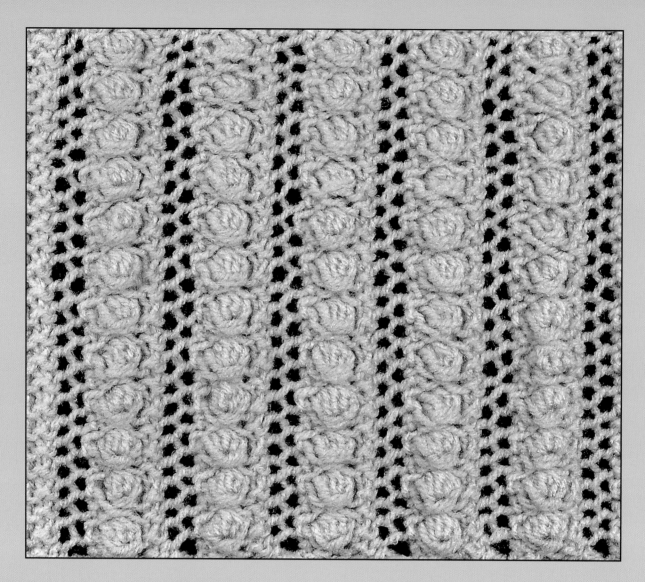

Lacy Bobbles

Multiple: 6+ 2

STITCH GUIDE

BB (Bobble): Work (K1, YO) twice, K1 into st; YF, turn, sl 5; YF, turn, K5; pass 4th, 3rd, 2nd and first sts on right-hand needle separately over the last st knitted. Push bobble in place.

INSTRUCTIONS

Row 1: K1; *sl 1, K2, YO, K2tog, K1; rep from * to last st, K1.

Row 2: Rep Row 1.

Row 3: Rep Row 1.

Row 4: K1; *BB, K2, YO, K2tog, K1; rep from * to last st, K1.

Repeat Rows 1 through 4 for pattern, ending by working Row 1.

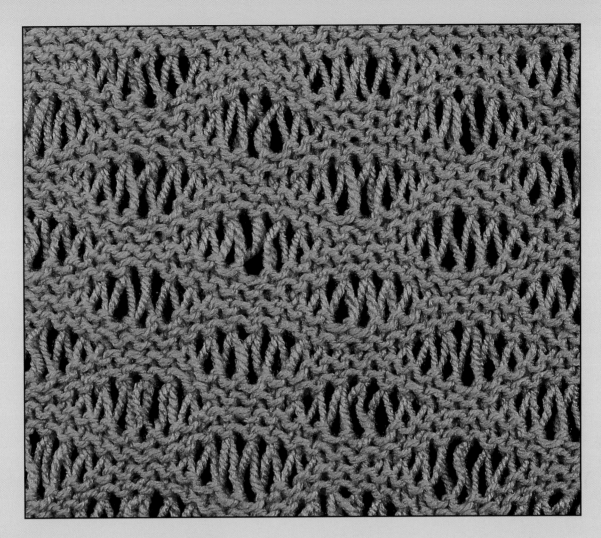

Wave Stitch

Multiple: 10 + 5

STITCH GUIDE

K1(W2): K1, wrapping yarn around needle twice.

K1(W3): K1, wrapping yarn around needle three times.

K1(W4): K1, wrapping yarn around needle four times.

INSTRUCTIONS

Row 1: Knit.

Row 2 (right side): Knit.

Row 3: K5; *K1(W2), K1(W3), K1(W4), K1(W3), K1(W2), K5; rep from * across.

Row 4: Knit, dropping wraps from needle.

Row 5: Knit.

Row 6: Knit.

Row 7: K1(W2), K1(W3), K1(W4), K1(W3), K1(W2); *K5, K1(W2), K1(W3), K1(W4), K1(W3), K1(W2), rep from * across.

Row 8: Repeat Row 4.

Repeat Rows 1 through 8 for pattern, ending with a Row 2 or Row 6.

Clusters

Multiple: 6 + 7

STITCH GUIDE

CL (Cluster): Sl 4 sts onto right needle, K1, pass each sl st separately over the knitted stitch: CL made.

M5 (Make 5): K1, K1tbl, YO, K1, K1tbl in same st: 5 worked in one st.

INSTRUCTIONS

Row 1: Knit.

Row 2: Knit.

Row 3 (right side): K4; *Cl, K1; rep from * to last 3 sts, K3.

Row 4: K1, YF, sl 3, YB; *M5, YF, sl 1, YB; rep from * to last 4 sts, YF, sl 3, YB, K1.

Row 5: Knit.

Row 6: Knit.

Row 7: K1, CL; *K1, CL; rep from * to first, K1.

Row 8: K1, M5; *YF, sl 1, YB, M5; rep from * to last st, K1.

Repeat Rows 1 through 8 for pattern, ending by working a Row 1.

Tri-Color

Multiple: 3 + 1

INSTRUCTIONS

Worked in three colors: *Color A, Color B, and Color C; carry unused color loosely along side edge of work.*

CO with A.

Row 1 (wrong side): With A, knit,

Row 2: With B, K3; *sl 1, K2; rep from * to last st, K1.

Row 3: With B, K3; *YF, sl 1, YB, K2; rep from * to last st, K1.

Row 4: With C; *K2, sl 1; rep from * to last st, K1.

Row 5: With C, K1; *YF, sl 1, YB, K2; rep from * to end.

Row 6: With A, K1; *sl 1, K2; rep from * to end.

Row 7: With A, *K2, YF, sl 1, YB, rep from * to last st, K1.

Repeat Rows 2 through 7 for pattern.

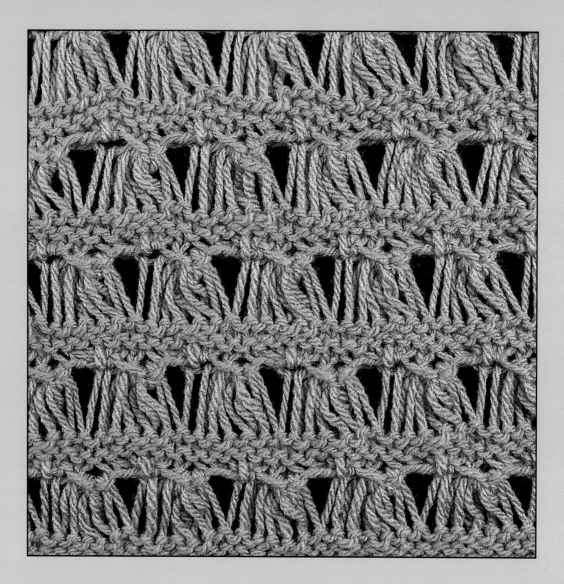

Haystacks

Multiple: 6 + 2

STITCH GUIDE

M5 (Make 5): K1, K1tbl, YO, K1, K1tbl in same st: 5 sts worked in same st.

P3SSO: Pass 3 slip sts over knit st.

K1(W3): K1, wrapping yarn around needle three times.

INSTRUCTIONS

Row 1: Knit.

Row 2 (right side): Knit.

Row 3: K1; *K1(W3), K1; rep from * to last st, K1.

Row 4: K1; *K1 drop YO, K1; rep from * to last st, K1.

Row 5: K1; *sl 3, K2tog, P3SSO, M5; rep from * to last st, K1.

Row 6: Knit.

Row 7: Knit.

Row 8: Knit.

Row 9: Rep Row 3,

Row 10: Rep Row 4.

Row 11: K1; *M5, sl 3, K2tog, P3SSO; rep from * to last st, K1.

Row 12: Knit.

Repeat Rows 1 through 12 for pattern.

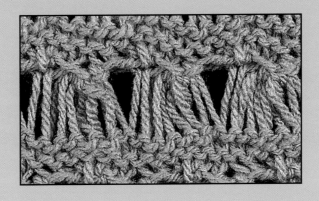

Chevrons

Multiple: 11 + 2

STITCH GUIDE

Inc (Increase): Knit into front lp, then back lp of st.

INSTRUCTIONS

Two colors: *Color A and Color B; carry unused color loosely along side.*

Rows 1 through 5: With A, knit.

Row 6 (right side): With B, K1; *K2tog, K2, (Inc) twice, K3, sl 1, K1, PSSO; rep from * to last st, K1.

Row 7: Knit.

Row 8: Rep Row 6.

Row 9: Knit.

Row 10: Rep Row 6.

Row 11: Knit.

Row 12: With A, K1; *K2tog, K2, (Inc) twice, K3, sl 1, K1, PSSO; rep from * to last st, K1.

Row 13: Knit.

Row 14: Rep Row 12.

Row 15: Knit.

Row 16: Rep Row 12.

Row 17: Knit.

Repeat Rows 6 through 17 until desired length is reached.

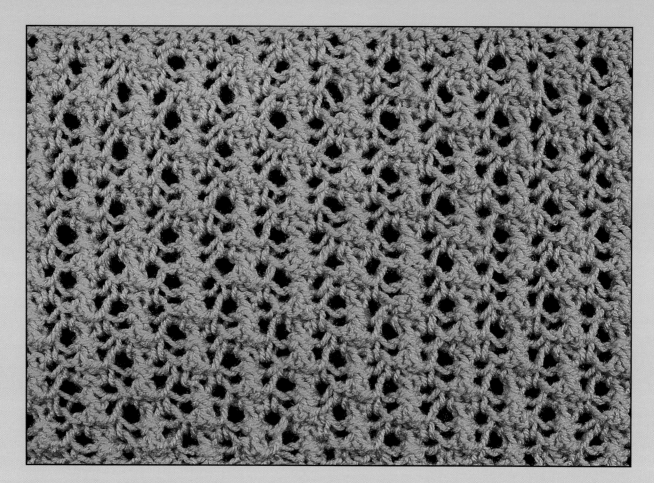

Leafy Lace

Multiple: 6 + 2

STITCH GUIDE

K1B (Knit 1 below): Insert needle into st below next st on left needle and knit it, slipping the st above off the needle at the same time.

INSTRUCTIONS

Row 1: Knit.

Row 2 (right side): K1; *K1B, K1, K1B, YO, K3tog, YO; rep from * to last st, K1.

Row 3: Knit.

Row 4: Rep Row 2.

Row 5: Knit.

Row 6: K1; *YO, K3tog, YO, K1B, K1, K1B; rep from * to last st, K1.

Row 7: Knit.

Row 8: Rep Row 6.

Row 9: Knit.

Repeat Rows 2 through 9 for pattern.

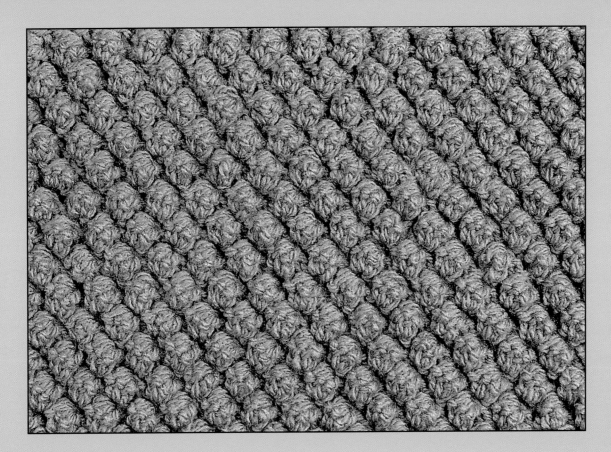

Berries

Multiple: 2 + 1

STITCH GUIDE

BB (Bobble): Work (K1, YO) twice, K1 into st; YF, turn, sl 5; YF, turn, K5; pass 4th, 3rd, 2nd and first sts on right-hand needle separately over the last st knitted. Push bobble in place.

INSTRUCTIONS

Row 1: K1; *BB, K1; rep from * across.

Row 2: Knit.

Row 3: K2; *BB, K1; rep from * across to last st, K1.

Row 4: Knit.

Repeat Rows 1 through 4 for pattern.

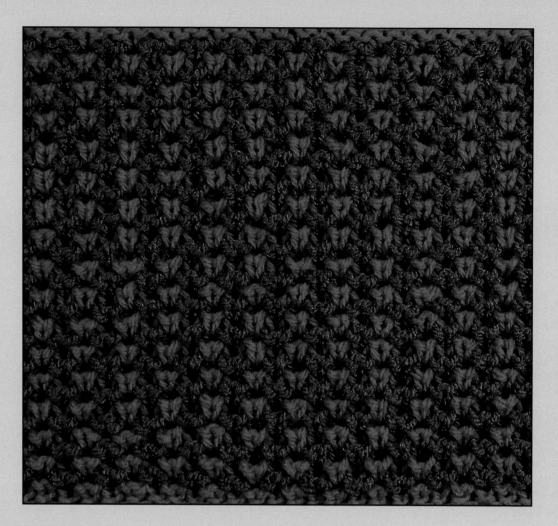

Brioche

Multiple: 2 + 5

STITCH GUIDE

K1B (Knit 1 below): Insert needle into st below next st on left needle and knit it, slipping the st above off the needle at the same time.

INSTRUCTIONS

Two colors: *Color A and Color B; carry unused color loosely along side edge of work.*

Row 1 (right side): With A, knit.

Row 2: With A, knit.

Row 3: With B, K3; *K1b, K1; rep from * to last 2 sts, K2.

Row 4: With B, knit.

Row 5: With A, K2, K1b; *K1, K1b; rep from * to last 2 sts, K2.

Row 6: With A, knit.

Repeat Rows 3 through 6 for pattern.

Slip and Slide

Multiple: 6 + 4

INSTRUCTIONS

Row 1 (right side): Knit.

Row 2: K1; *YF, sl 2, YB, K4; rep from * to last 3 sts, YF, sl 2, YB, K1.

Row 3: K1; *YB, sl 2, K4; rep from * to last 3 sts, sl 2, K1.

Row 4: K1; *YF, sl 2, YB, K4; rep from * to last 3 sts, YF, sl 2, YB, K1.

Row 5: K1; *YB, sl 2, K4; rep from * to last 3 sts, sl 2, K1.

Row 6: Rep Row 2.

Row 7: Knit.

Row 8: K4; *YF, sl 2, YB, K4; rep from * across.

Row 9: K4; *YB, sl 2, K4; rep from * across.

Row 10: K4; *YF, sl 2, YB, K4; rep from * across.

Row 11: K4; *YB, sl 2, K4; rep from * across.

Row 12: Rep Row 8.

Repeat Rows 1 through 12 for pattern.

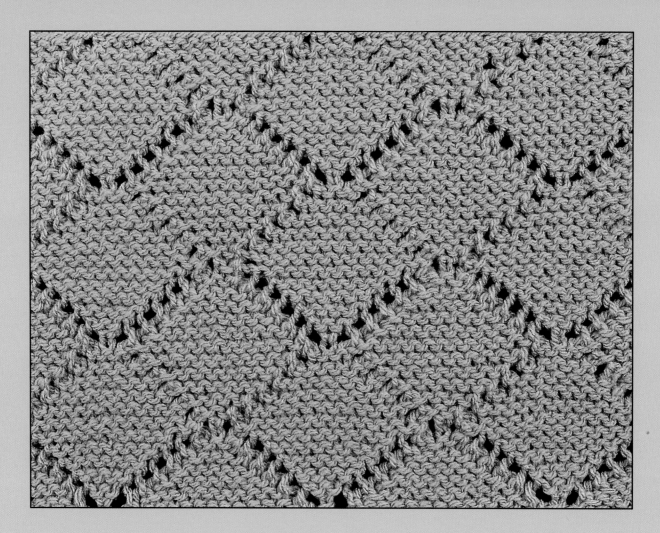

Lozenges

Multiple: 16 + 1

INSTRUCTIONS

Row 1: *K6, K2tog, YO, K1, YO, K2tog, K5; rep from * to last st, K1.

Row 2 and all even rows (right side): Knit.

Row 3: *K5, K2tog, YO, K3, YO, K2tog, K4; rep from * to last st, K1.

Row 5: *K4, K2tog, YO, K5, YO, K2tog, K3; rep from * to last st, K1.

Row 7: *K3, K2tog, YO, K7, YO, K2tog, K2; rep from * to last st, K1.

Row 9: *K2, K2tog, YO, K9, YO, K2tog, K1; rep from * to last st, K1.

Row 11: *K1, K2tog YO, K11, YO, K2tog; rep from * to last st, K1.

Row 13: *K1, YO, K2tog, K11, K2tog, YO; rep from * to last st, K1.

Row 15: Rep Row 11.

Row 17: Rep Row 9.

Row 19: Rep Row 7.

Row 21: Rep Row 5.

Row 23: Rep Row 3.

Row 24: Rep Row 2.

Repeat Rows 1 through 24 for pattern.

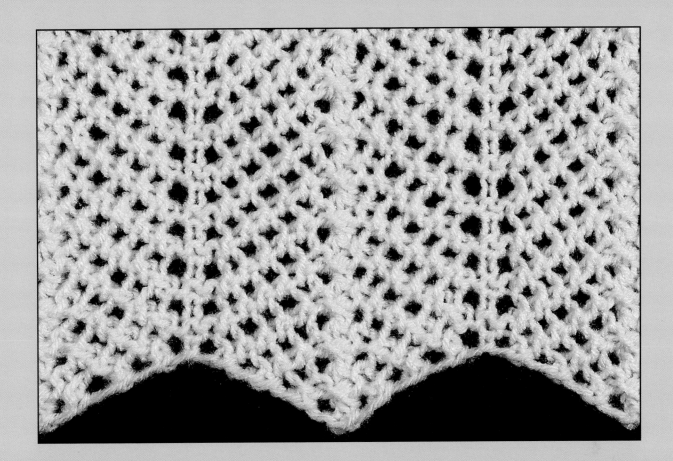

Lattice

Multiple: 16 + 2

STITCH GUIDE

P2SSO: Pass 2 sl sts over knit st.

INSTRUCTIONS

Row 1 (wrong side): K1; *K1, (YO, sl 1, K1, PSSO) 3 times, YO, sl 2, K1, P2SSO, (YO, K2tog) 3 times, YO; rep from * to last st, K1.

Row 2 (right side): Knit.

Row 3: K1; *K2, (YO, sl 1, K1, PSSO) twice, YO, K1, sl 2, K1, P2SSO, K1, (YO, K2tog) twice, YO, K1; rep from * to last st, K1.

Row 4: Knit.

Repeat Rows 1 through 4 for pattern.

Blue Bells

Multiple: 9 + 3

INSTRUCTIONS

Row 1: Knit.

Row 2: K2; *YF, sl 8, YB, K1; rep from * to last st, K1.

Row 3: K2; *YO, K8, YO, K1; rep from * to last st, K1.

Row 4: K3; *YF, sl 8, YB, K3; rep from * across.

Row 5: Knit.

Row 6: K3; *YF, sl 8, YB, K3; rep from * across.

Row 7: K3; *YO, K8, YO, K3; rep from * across.

Row 8: K4; *YF, sl 8, YB, K5; rep from * to last 4 sts, K4.

Row 9: Knit.

Row 10: K4; *YF, sl 8, YB, K5; rep from * to last 4 sts, K4.

Row 11: K4; *YO, K8, YO, K5; rep from * to last 4 sts, K4.

Row 12: K5; *YF, sl 8, YB, K7; rep from * to last 5 sts, K5.

Row 13: K5; *K4tog tbl, K4tog, K7; rep from * to last 5 sts, K5.

Row 14: K5; *YF, sl 2, YB, K7; rep from * to last 5 sts, K5.

Repeat Rows 1 through 14, ending by working Row 1.

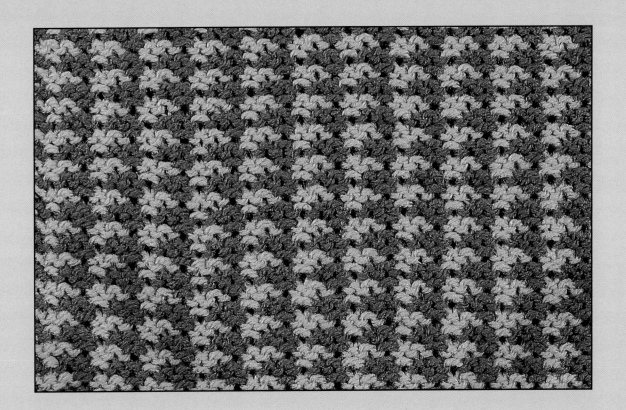

Checkers

Multiple 3 + 2

INSTRUCTIONS

Two colors: *Color A and Color B; carry un-used color loosely along side edge of work.*

Row 1: With Color A, knit.

Row 2 (right side): With Color B, K1; *K2, sl 1; rep from * to last st, K1.

Row 3: With Color B, knit.

Row 4: With Color A, K1; *sl 1, K2; rep from * to last st, K1.

Row 5: With Color A, knit.

Repeat Rows 2 through 5 for pattern.

Checks and Balances

Multiple 16 + 2

INSTRUCTONS

Row 1 (right side): K1; *(sl 1, K1, PSSO, YO) 4 times, K8; rep from * to last st, K1.

Row 2: K1; *K8, YF, sl 8, YB; rep from * to last st, K1.

Row 3: K1; *(sl 1, K1, PSSO, YO) 4 times, K8; rep from * to last st, K1.

Row 4: K1; *K8, YF, sl 8, YB; rep from * to last st, K1.

Row 5: K1; *(sl 1, K1, PSSO, YO) 4 times, K8; rep from * to last st, K1

Row 6: K1; *K8, YF, sl 8, YB; rep from * to last st, K1.

Row 7: K1; *(sl 1, K1, PSSO, YO) 4 times, K8; rep from * to last st, K1.

Row 8: K1; *K8, YF, sl 8, YB; rep from * to last st, K1.

Row 9: K1; *K8, (YO, K2tog) 4 times; rep from * to last st, K1.

Row 10: K1; *YF, sl 8, YB, K8; rep from * to last st, K1.

Row 11: K1; *K8, (YO, K2tog) 4 times; rep from * to last st, K1.

Row 12: K1; *YF, sl 8, YB, K8; rep from * to last st, K1.

Row 13: K1; *K8, (YO, K2tog) 4 times; rep from * to last st, K1.

Row 14: K1; *YF, sl 8, YB, K8; rep from * to last st, K1.

Row 15: K1; *K8, (YO, K2tog) 4 times; rep from * to last st, K1.

Row 16: K1; *YF, sl 8, YB, K8; rep from * to last st, K1.

Repeat Rows 1 through 16 for pattern.

Climbing Ropes

Multiple: 6 + 5

INSTRUCTIONS

Row 1: (K1, sl 1) twice; *YO, K3tog, YO, sl 1, K1, sl 1; rep from * to last st, K1.

Row 2: K2, YF, sl 1, YB, K1; *YF, sl 3, YB, K1, YF, sl 1, YB, K1; rep from * to last st, K1.

Row 3: (K1, sl 1) twice; *K3, sl 1, K1, sl 1; rep from * to last st, K1.

Row 4: K2, YF, sl 1, YB, K1; *YF, sl 3, YB, K1, YF, sl 1, YB, K1; rep from * to last st, K1.

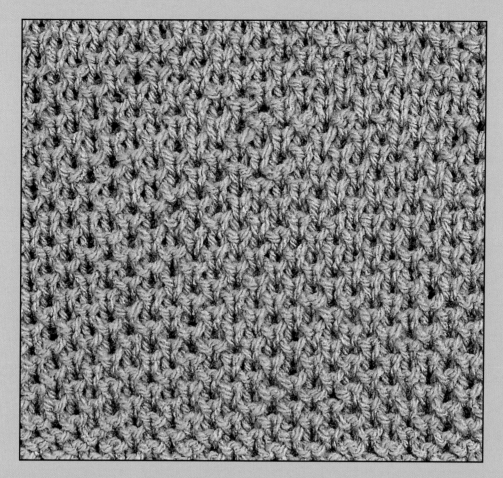

Traveling Brioche

Multiple: 2 + 1

STITCH GUIDE

K1B (Knit 1 below): Insert needle into st below next st on left needle and knit it, slipping the st above off the needle at the same time.

INSTRUCTIONS

Row 1 (wrong side): Knit.

Row 2: K1; *K1B, K1; rep from * across.

Row 3: Knit.

Row 4: K2, K1B; *K1, K1B; rep from * to last 2 sts, K2.

Repeat Rows 1 through 4 for pattern.

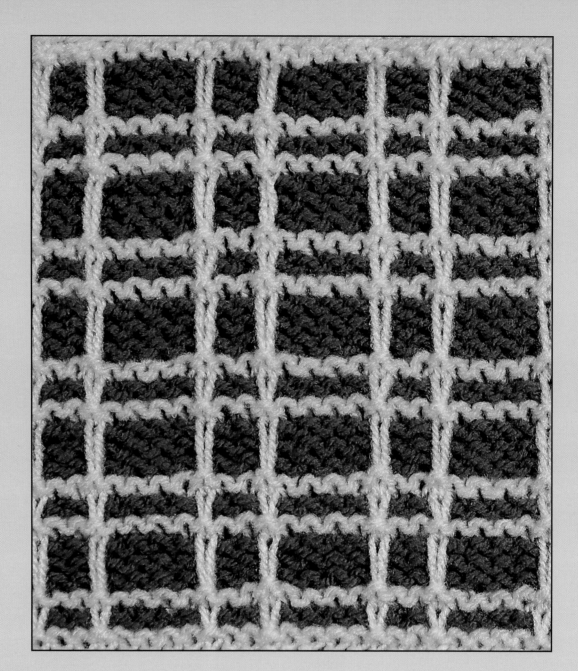

Plaid

Multiple: 8 + 6

STITCH GUIDE

K1(W2): K1, wrapping yarn twice around needle

INSTRUCTIONS

Two colors: *Color A and Color B; carry unused color loosely along side edge of work.*

Row 1 (right side): With A, knit.

Row 2: Knit.

Row 3: With B, K1, sl 1, K2, sl 1; *K4, sl 1, K2, sl 1; rep from * to last st, K1.

Row 4: With B, K1, YF, sl 1, YB, K2, YF, sl 1, *YB, K4, YF, sl 1, YB, K2, YF, sl 1; rep from * to last st, YB, K1.

Row 5: With A, knit.

Row 6: With A, K1, K1(W2), K2, K1(W2); *K4, K1(W2), K2, K1(W2); rep from * to last st, K1.

Row 7: With B, K1, sl 1, allowing lps to drop, K2, sl 1, allowing lps to drop; *K4, sl 1, allowing lps to drop, K2, sl 1, allowing lps to drop; rep from * to last st, K1.

Row 8: Rep Row 4.

Row 9: Rep Row 3.

Row 10: Rep Row 4.

Row 11: Rep Row 3.

Row 12: Rep Row 4.

Repeat Rows 1 through 12 for pattern, ending with Row 2.

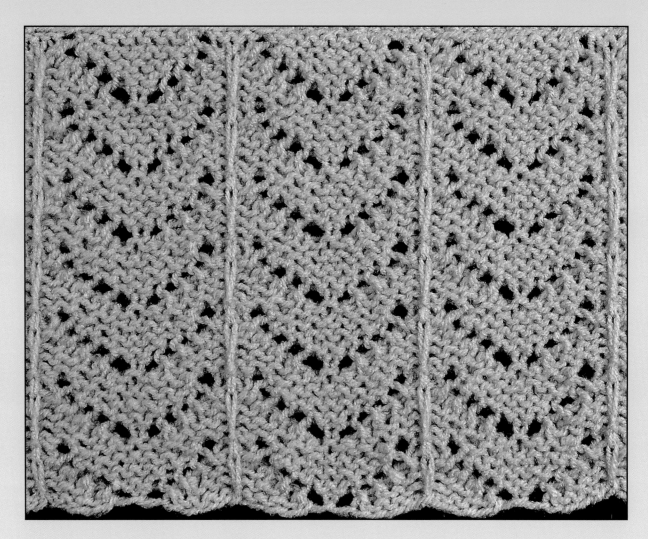

Arrowheads

Multiple: 12 + 2

STITCH GUIDE

K1tbl: Knit into back lp of st.

INSTRUCTIONS

Row 1: K1; *YO, sl 1, K1, PSSO, K3, YF, sl 1, YB, K3, K2tog, YO, K1; rep from * to last st, K1.

Row 2 (right side): K1; *K2, K1tbl, K3, sl 1, K3, K1tbl, K1; rep from * to last st, K1.

Row 3: K1; *K1, YO, sl 1, K1, PSSO, K2, YF, sl 1, YB, K2, K2tog, YO, K2; rep from * to last st, K1.

Row 4: K1; *K3, K1tbl, K2, sl l, K2, K1tbl, K2; rep from * to last st, K1.

Row 5: K1; *K2, YO, sl 1, K1, PSSO, K1, YF, sl 1, YB, K1, K2tog, YO, K3; rep from * to last st, K1.

Row 6: K1; *K4, K1tbl, K1, sl 1, K1, K1tbl, K3; rep from * to last st, K1.

Row 7: K1; *K3, YO, sl 1, K1, PSSO, YF, sl l, YB, K2tog, YO, K4; rep from * to last st, K1.

Row 8: K1; *K1tbl, K4, (K1tbl) 3 times, K4; rep from * to last st, K1.

Row 9: K1; *K2, K2tog, YO, K3, YO, K2tog, K3; rep from * to last st, K1.

Row 10: K1; *K1, K1tbl, K4, sl 1, K4, K1tbl; rep from * to last st, K1.

Repeat Rows 1 through 10 for pattern.

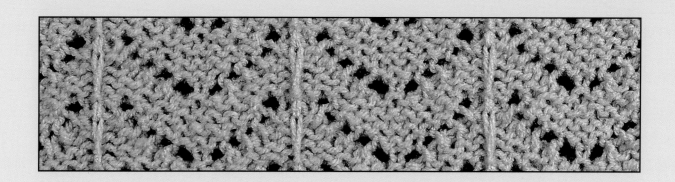

Open Ribs

Multiple: 2 sts

INSTRUCTIONS

Row 1: K1; *YO, sl 1, K1; rep from * across, ending with K1.

Row 2 (right side): K2; *K2tog, K1; rep from * across.

Repeat Rows 1 and 2 for pattern.

Slanting Bobbles

Multiple: 5 + 2

STITCH GUIDE

BB (Bobble): Work (K1, YO) twice, K1 into st; YF, turn, sl 5; YF, turn, K5; pass 4th, 3rd, 2nd and first sts on right-hand needle separately over the last st knitted. Push bobble in place.

INSTRUCTIONS

Row 1: K5, BB; *K4, BB; rep from * to last st, K1.

Row 2 and all even rows: Knit.

Row 3: *K4, BB; rep from * to last 2 sts, K2.

Row 5: K3, BB; *K4, BB; rep from * to last 3 sts, K3.

Row 7: K2; *BB, K4; rep from * across.

Row 9: K1; *BB, K4; rep from * to last st, K1.

Row 10: Rep Row 2.

Repeat Rows 1 through 10 for pattern.

Two-Color Stripe

Multiple: 2 sts

INSTRUCTIONS

Two colors: *Color A & Color B; carry unused color loosely along side edge of work.*

Row 1 (right side): With color A, Knit.

Row 2: Knit.

Row 3: K1; *YB, sl 1, K1; rep from * to last st, K1.

Row 4: K1; *YB, K1, YF, sl 1; rep from * to last st, YB, K1. Drop Color A.

Row 5: With Color B, knit.

Row 6: Knit.

Row 7: K1; *YF, sl 1, YB, K1; rep from * to last st, K1.

Row 8: K1; *K1, YB, sl 1; rep from * to last st, K1. Drop Color B.

Repeat Rows 1 through 8 for pattern.

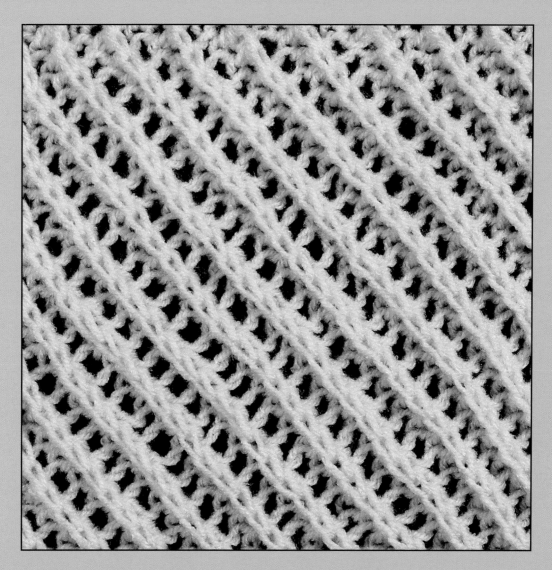

Diagonal Openwork

Multiple: 4

INSTRUCTIONS

Row 1 (right side): K1; *K1, YO, sl 1, K2tog, PSSO, YO; rep from to last 3 sts, K3.

Row 2: K1, YF, sl 2, YB; *K1, YF, sl 1, YB; rep from * to last st, K1.

Row 3: K3; *YO, sl 1, K2tog, PSSO, YO, K1; rep from * to last st, K1.

Row 4: K1; *YF, sl 1, YB, K1; rep from * to last 3 sts, YF, sl 2, YB, K1.

Row 5: K1, K2tog, YO, K1, YO; *sl 1, K2tog, PSSO, YO, K1, YO, rep from * to last 4 sts, sl 1, K1, PSSO, K2.

Row 6: K1, YF, sl 2; *K1, YF, sl 1, YB; rep from * to last st, K1.

Row 7: K2, K2tog, YO, K1, YO, *sl 1, K2tog, PSSO, YO, K1, YO; rep to last 3 sts, sl 1, K1, PSSO, K1.

Row 8: K1, YF, sl 1, YB; *K1, YF, sl 1, YB; rep from * to last 2 sts, K2.

Repeat Rows 1 through 8 for pattern.

Honeycomb

Multiple: 3

INSTRUCTIONS

With two colors: *Color A and Color B; carry unused yarn loosely along side edge of work.*

Row 1: With A, knit.

Row 2: With A, K2; *YO, sl 1, K2, PSSO knit sts; rep from * to last st, K1.

Row 3: With B, knit.

Row 4: With B, K1; *sl 1, K2, PSSO knit sts, YO; rep from * to last 2 sts, K2.

Rep Row 1 through 4 for pattern.

Dotted Lines

Multiple: 4 + 2

INSTRUCTIONS

Two colors: *Color A and Color B; carry unused color loosely along wrong side of work until needed.*

Row 1 (right side): *With color A, K2; wth color B, K2; rep from * to last 2sts, with A, K2.

Row 2: With A, K1; * with A, YO, K2, pass YO over; with B, YO, K2, pass YO over; rep from * to last st, with A, K1.

Row 3: *With B, K2; with A, K2; rep from * to last 2 sts, with B, K2.

Row 4: With B, K1, *with B, YO, K2, pass YO over, with A, YO, K2, pass YO over; rep from * to last st, with B, K1.

Repeat Rows 1 through 4 for pattern

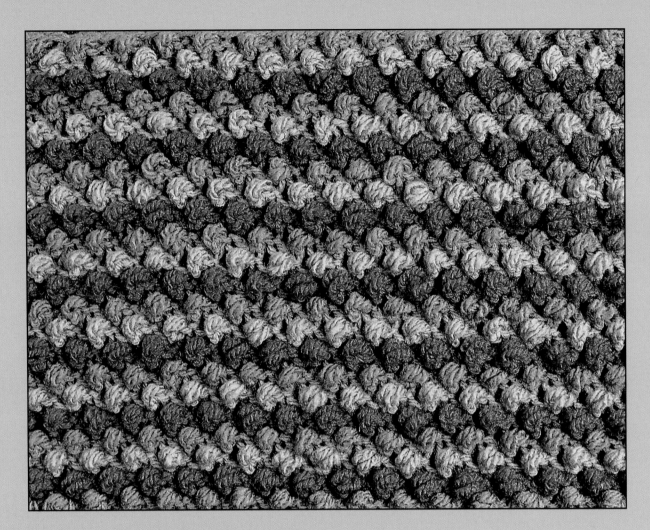

Tiny Bobbles

Multiple: 2 + 1

STITCH GUIDE

BB (Bobble): Work (K1, K1tbl) twice all in next st, pass 3rd, 2nd and first sts over last st made.

Three Colors: *Color A, Color B and Color C; carry unused color loosely along side edge of work.*

INSTRUCTIONS

Row 1 (right side): With A, knit.

Row 2: With A, K1; *BB, K1; rep from * across.

Row 3: With B, knit.

Row 4: With B, K2; *BB, K1; rep from * to last st, K1.

Row 5: With C, knit.

Row 6: With C, K1; *BB, K1; rep from * across.

Row 7: With A, knit.

Row 8: With A, K2; *BB, K1; rep from * to last st, K1.

Row 9: With B, knit.

Row 10: With B, K1; *BB, K1; rep from * across.

Row 11: With C, knit.

Row 12: With C, K2; *BB, K1; rep from * to last st, K1.

Repeat Rows 1 through 12 for pattern.

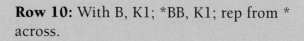

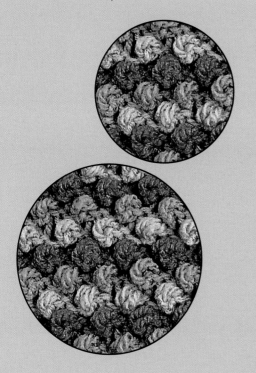

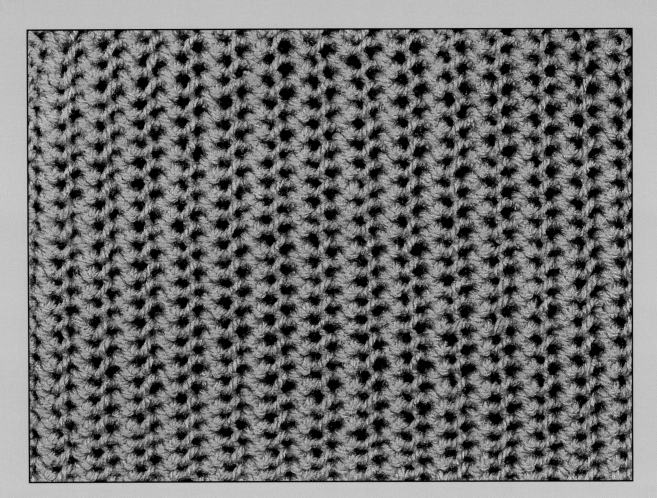

Mesh

Multiple 2 + 2

INSTRUCTIONS

Row 1: K1; *YO, sl 1, K1, PSSO; rep from * to last st, K1.

Repeat Row 1 for pattern.

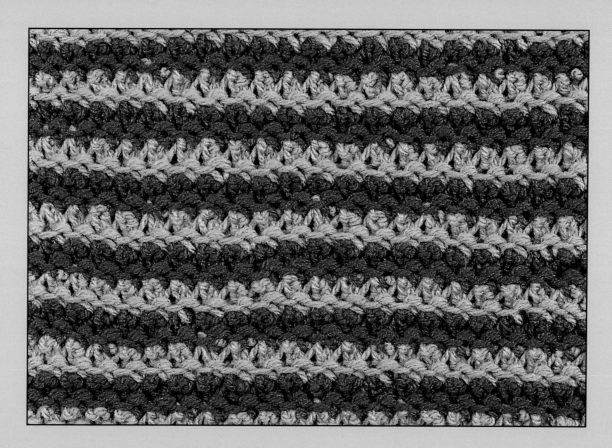

Textured Ridges

Multiple: 2

STITCH GUIDE

K1B (Knit 1 below): Insert needle into st below next st on left needle and knit it, slipping the st above off the needle at the same time.

INSTRUCTIONS

Two colors: *Color A and Color B; carry un-used color loosely along side edge of work.*

Foundation Row: With Color A, Knit.

Row 1 (right side): With Color A, K1; *K1B, K1; rep from * to last st, K1.

Row 2: K1; *K2tog; rep from * to last st, K1.

Row 3: K1; *Knit into front and back of next st, rep from * to last st, K1.

Row 4: Knit.

Row 5: With Color B, rep Row 1.

Row 6: Rep Row 2.

Row 7: Rep Row 3.

Row 8: Rep Row 4.

Repeat Rows 1 through 8, changing color where necessary.

Cardigan Stitch

Multiple: 3 + 2

INSTRUCTIONS

Note: *Slip all stitches from right to left.*

Row 1: K1; *YO, sl 1, K2tog; rep from * across ending with K1.

Repeat Row 1 for pattern.

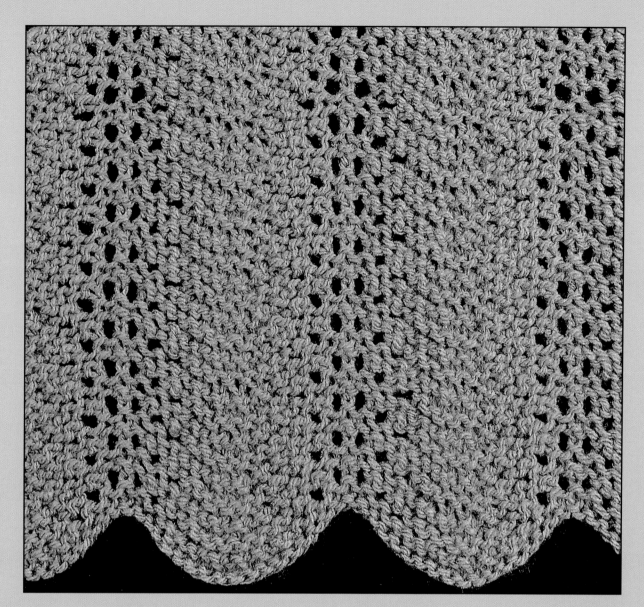

Lace Ripple

Multiple 18 + 2

INSTRUCTIONS

Row 1 (right side): Knit.

Row 2: Knit

Row 3: K1; *(K2tog) 3 times, (YO, K1) 6 times; (K2tog) 3 times; rep from * to last st, K1.

Row 4: Knit.

Repeat Rows 1 through 4 for pattern.

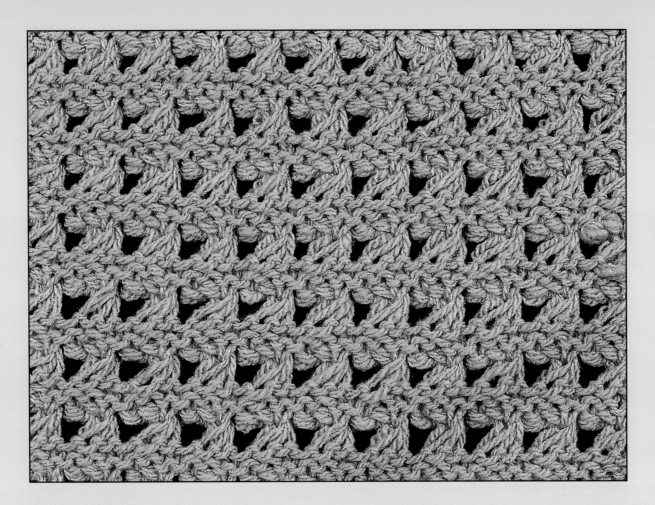

Eyelets

Multiple: 3 + 2

INSTRUCTIONS

Row 1 (right side): Knit.

Row 2: K1; *K1, (YO) 3 times; rep from * to last st, K1.

Row 3: K1; *(drop 3 YOs, sl 1) 3 times: 3 long sts. Sl 3 long sts to left needle and knit them tog tbl, then knit through front lp, and finally knit them tog tbl; rep from * to last st, K1.

Row 4: Knit.

Repeat Rows 1 through 4 for pattern.

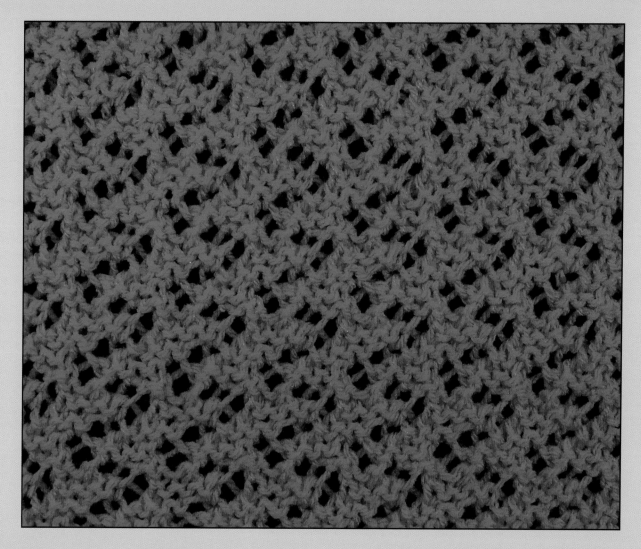

Zigzag Lace

Multiple: 5 + 2

INSTRUCTIONS

Row 1: K1; *K2, K2tog, YO, K1; rep from * to last st, K1.

Row 2 (right side): K1; *K2, YO, K2tog, K1; rep from * to last st, K1.

Row 3: K1; *K2tog, YO, K3; rep from * to last st, K1.

Row 4: K1; *K2tog, K3, YO; rep from * to last st, K1.

Row 5: K1; *YO, sl 1, K1, PSSO, K3; rep from * to last st, K1.

Row 6: K1; *K2, sl 1, K1, PSSO, YO, K1; rep from * to last st, K1.

Row 7: K1; *K2, YO, sl 1, K1, PSSO, K1; rep from * to last st, K1.

Row 8: K1; *sl 1, K1, PSSO, YO, K3; rep from * to last st, K1.

Repeat Rows 1 through 8 for pattern.

Polka Dots

Multiple 2 + 1

INSTRUCTIONS

Two colors: *Color A and Color B; carry unused color loosely along side edge of work.*

Row 1 (right side): With Color A, K1; *sl 1, K1; rep from * across.

Row 2: K1; *YF, sl 1, YB, K1; rep from * across.

Row 3: With Color B, K2, *sl 1, K1; rep from * to last st, K1.

Row 4: K2; *YF, sl 1, YB, KI; rep from * to last st, K1.

Repeat Rows 1 through 4 for pattern.

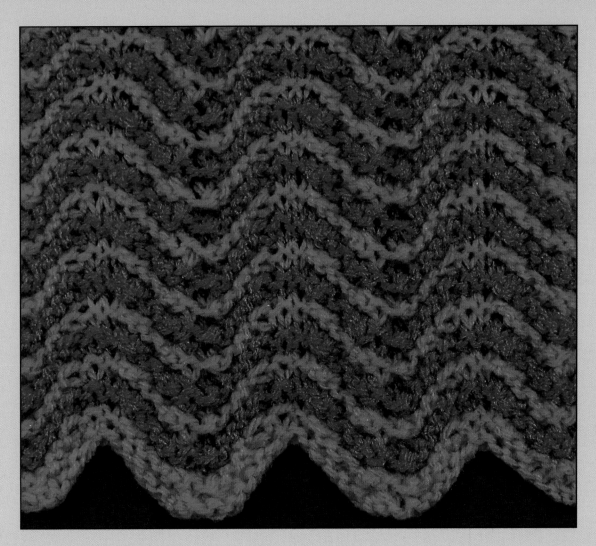

Crested Waves

Multiple: 14+ 2

STITCH GUIDE

M3 (Make 3): K1, K1tbl, K1 in next st: 3 sts worked in one st.

INSTRUCTIONS

Two Colors: *Color A and Color B; carry unused color loosely along side edge of work.*

Row 1: With color A: K1, *K3tog, K5, M3, K5; rep from * to last st, K1.

Row 2: K1; *K3tog, K5, M3, K5; rep from * to last st, K1.

Row 3: With Color B: Rep Row 1.

Row 4: Rep Row 2.

Rep Rows 1 through 4 for pattern.

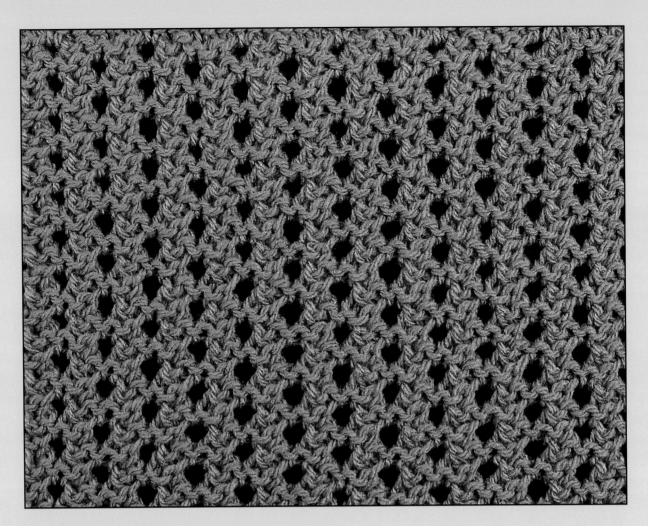

Traveling Eyelet

Multiple: 6 + 8

STITCH GUIDE

Inc (Increase): Knit into front lp, then back lp of st.

INSTRUCTIONS

Row 1: K1, YO, sl 1, K1, PSSO, K2; *K2tog, YO, sl 1, K1, PSSO, K2; rep from * to last 3 sts, K2tog, YO, K1.

Row 2 (right side): K2; *K4, Inc in YO, rep from * to last 6 sts, K6.

Row 3: K2; *K2tog, YO, sl 1, K1, PSSO, K2; rep from * across.

Row 4: K3; *Inc in YO, K4, rep from * to last 4 sts, Inc, K3.

Openwork

Multiple 3 + 2

INSTRUCTIONS

Row 1: K1; *YO, sl 1, K2, PSSO the K2; rep from * to last st, K1.

Row 2 (right side): Knit.

Intermesh

Multiple: 3

INSTRUCTIONS

Row 1: K2; *YO, K3, pass first knit stitch of K3 over second and third sts; rep from * to last st, K1.

Row 2 (right side): Knit.

Row 3: K1; *K3, pass first knit stitch of K3 over second and third sts, YO; rep from * to last 2 sts, K2.

Row 4: Knit.

Repeat Rows 1 through 4 for pattern.

Springtime Lace

Multiple: 11 + 2

INSTRUCTIONS

Row 1 (right side): K1; *sl 1, K1, PSSO, K3tbl, YO, K1, YO, K3tbl, K2tog; rep from * to last st, K1.

Row 2: K1; *YF, sl 4, YB, K3, YF, sl 4, rep from * to last st, K1.

Row 3: K1, *sl 1, K1, PSSO, K2tbl, YO, K1, YO, sl 1, K1, PSSO, YO, K2tbl, K2tog; rep from * to last st, K1.

Row 4: K1; *YF, sl 3, YB, K5, YF, sl 3; rep from * to last st, K1.

Row 5: K1; *sl 1, K1, PSSO, K1tbl, YO, K1, (YO, sl 1, K1, PSSO) twice, YO, K1tbl, K2tog; rep from * to last st, K1.

Row 6: Rep row 4.

Row 7: K1; *sl 1, K1, PSSO, YO, K1, (YO, sl 1, K1, PSSO) three times, YO, K2tog; rep from * to last st, K1.

Row 8: K1; *YF, sl 2, YB, K7, YF, sl 2; rep from * to last st, K1.

Repeat rows 1 through 8 for pattern.

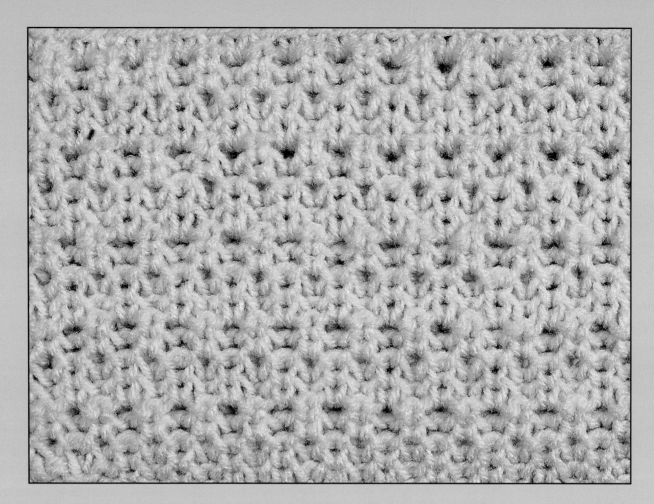

Fisherman's Rib

Multiple: 2+1

STITCH GUIDE

K1B (Knit 1 below): Insert needle into st below next st on left needle and knit it, slipping the st above off the needle at the same time.

INSTRUCTIONS

Foundation Row: Knit.

Row 1 (right side): Sl 1, *K1B, K1; rep from * across

Row 2: Sl 1; *K1, K1B; rep from * to last 2 sts, K2.

Row 3: Rep Row 1.

Row 4: Rep Row 2.

Row 5: Rep Row 1.

Row 6: Sl 1; *K1B, K1; rep from * across.

Row 7: Rep Row 2.

Row 8: Rep Row 6.

Row 9: Rep Row 2.

Row 10: Rep Row 6.

Repeat Rows 1 through 10 for pattern.

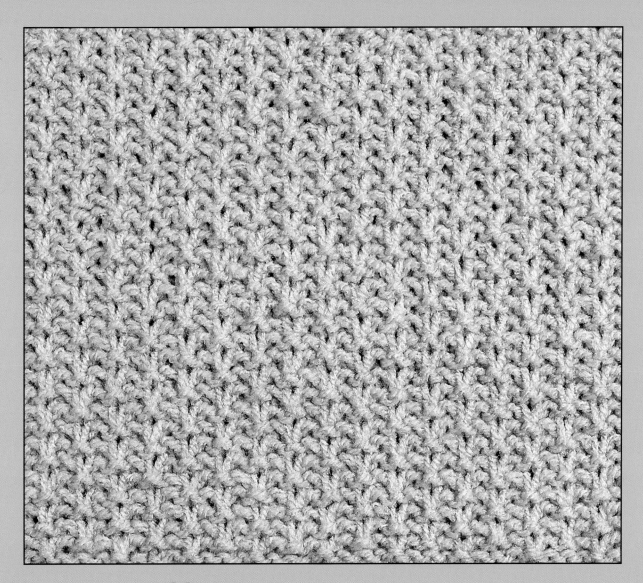

Vertical Visions

Multiple: 4 + 3

INSTRUCTIONS

Row 1 (right side): K3; *YB, sl 1, K3; rep from * across.

Row 2: K3; *YF, Sl 1, YB, K3; rep from * across.

Row 3: K1; *YB, sl 1, K3; rep from * to last 2 sts, YB, sl 1, K1.

Row 4: K1; *YF, sl 1, YB, K3 rep from * to last 2 sts, YF, sl 1, YB, K1.

Rep Rows 1 through 4 for pattern.

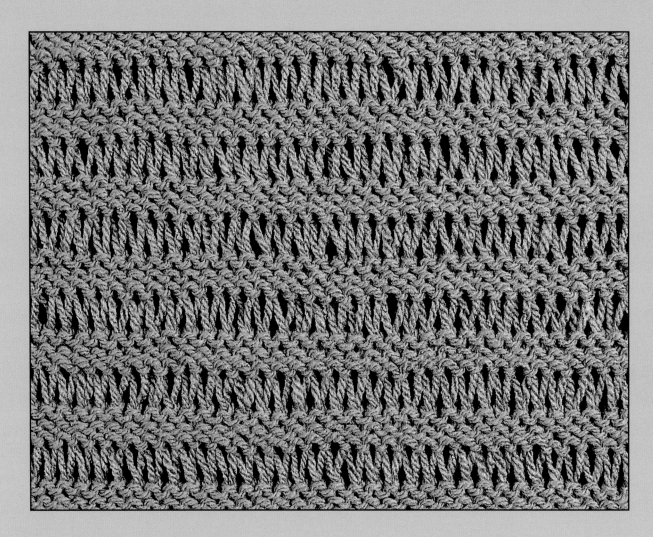

Drop Stitch

Multiple: Any uneven number.

STITCH GUIDE

K1(W2): K1, wrapping yarn twice around needle.

INSTRUCTIONS

Row 1: Knit.

Row 2: Knit.

Row 3: Knit.

Row 4: Knit.

Row 5: *K1, K1(W2); rep from * to last st, K1.

Row 6: *K1, K1 dropping YO from needle; rep from * to last st, K1.

Repeat Rows 1 through 6 for pattern, ending with Row 4.

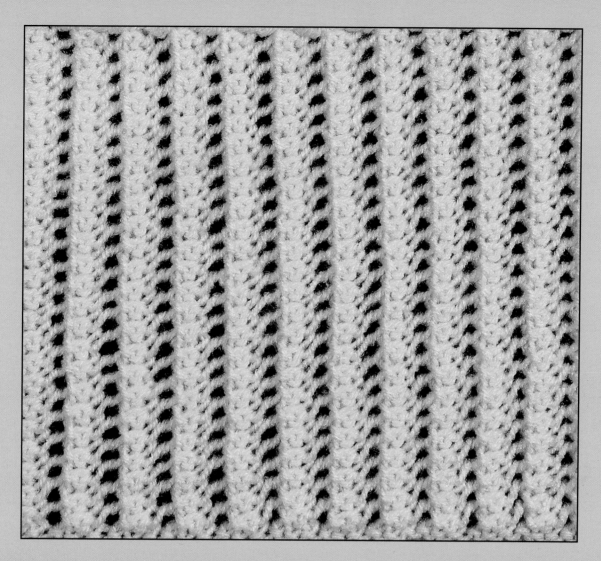

Eyelet Columns

Multiple 3 + 2

INSTRUCTIONS

Row 1 (right side): Knit.

Row 2: K1; *YO, sl 1, K2, PSSO the K2; rep from * to last st, K1.

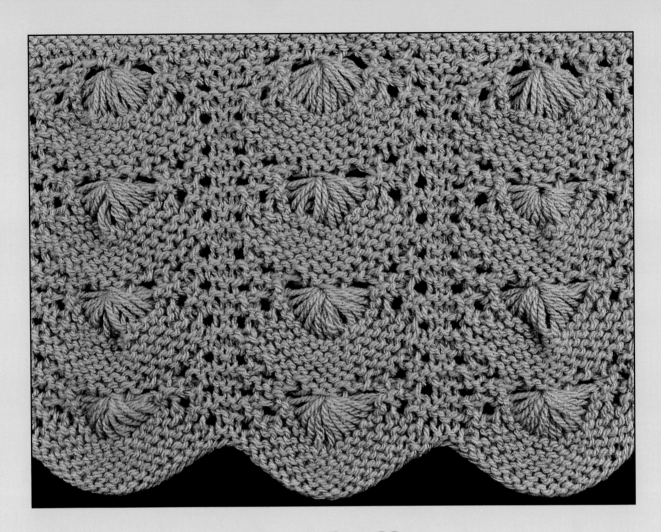

Garter Cockle Shells

Multiple: 19 + 2

INSTRUCTIONS

Row 1: Knit.

Row 2: Knit.

Row 3: K1; *K1, YO, K2tog, K13, K2tog, YO, K1; rep from * to last st, K1.

Row 4 (right side): K1; *K1, work (K1, K1tbl) into YO, K15, work (K1, K1tbl) into YO, K1; rep from * to last st: 21 sts each repeat.

Row 5: Knit.

Row 6: Knit.

Row 7: K1; *K1, (YO, K2tog) twice, K11, (K2tog, YO) twice, K1; rep from * to last st, K1.

Row 8: K1; *[K1, work (K1, K1tbl) into YO] twice, K13, (K1, K1tbl into YO, K1) twice; rep from * to last st, K2: 25 sts each repeat.

Row 9: Knit.

Row 10: K1; *K6, [(YO) twice, K1] 14 times, K5; rep from * to last st, K1: 53 sts each repeat.

Row 11: K1; *K1, (YO, K2tog) twice, YO, sl next 15 sts to right-hand needle, allowing extra lps to drop. Sl these 15 sts back onto left-hand needle and knit all 15 sts tog; (YO, K2tog) twice, YO, K1; rep from * to last st, K1: 13 sts each repeat.

Row 12: K1; *[K1, (K1, K1tbl into YO)] three times, K1, [(K1, K1tbl into YO),K1] three times; rep from * to last st, K1.

Row 13: Knit.

Repeat Rows 2 through 13 for pattern.

General Directions

ABBREVIATIONS AND SYMBOLS

Knit patterns are written in a special shorthand, which is used so that instructions don't take up too much space. They sometimes seem confusing, but once you learn them, you'll have no trouble following them.

These are Standard Abbreviations

BB	bobble
BO	bind off
CO	cast on
CL	cluster
Dec	decrease
Inc	increase(ing)
K	knit
K1b	knit 1 below
Ktbl	knit through the back loop
K2tog	knit two stitches together
K3tog	knit three stitches togeher
K4tog	knit four stitches together
Lp(s)	loop(s)
M3	Work 3 sts in one st
M5	Work 5 sts in one st
Patt	pattern
Prev	previous
PSSO	pass the slipped stitch over
P2SSO	pass two slipped stitches over
P3SSO	pass three slipped stitches over
P4SSO	pass four slipped stitches over
Rem	remain(ing)
Rep	repeat(ing)
Sl	slip; always slip from right to left
St(s)	stitch(es)
Tbl	through back loop
Tog	together
W	wrap yarn around needle
YB	with yarn in back
YF	with yarn in front
YO	Yarn over the needle

These are Standard Symbols

* An asterisk (or double asterisks**) in a pattern row, indicates a portion of instructions to be used more than once. For instance, "rep from * three times" means that after working the instructions once, you must work them again three times for a total of 4 times in all.

( ) Parentheses enclose instructions which are to be worked the number of times following the parentheses. For instance, "(sl 1, K1) 3 times" means that you slip one stitch and then knit one stitch, three times.

[ ] Brackets are used in the same way as parentheses especially when there is more than one set of repeats such as [K1, work (K1, K1 tbl) into YO] twice.